AMPLIFY
MY
JOB SEARCH

Also by Jeffrey S. Ton

BOOKS

Amplify Your Job Search
https://jeffreyston.com/author-amplify-your-job-search

Amplify Your Value
https://jeffreyston.com/author-amplify-your-value

BLOGS

Rivers of Thought
https://riversofthought.net

People Development Magazine
https://peopledevelopmentmagazine.com/author/jeff-ton

Intel IT Peer Network
https://itpeernetwork.intel.com/author/jtongici

Institute for Digital Transformation
https://www.institutefordigitaltransformation.org/digital-era-now

Forbes Technology Council
https://www.forbes.com/sites/forbestechcouncil/people/jeffreyton

AMPLIFY
MY
JOB SEARCH

The Companion Workbook to
Amplify Your Job Search

Jeffrey S. Ton

Published by Ton Enterprises, LLC

Cover Design: Jennifer Vogel
Interior Design: Lori Paximadis
Graphic Design: Jennifer Vogel
Amplify Dial Image: Copyright © Le Moal Olivier

Trade Paper ISBN: 978-1-7353090-3-3

Contents

How to Use This Workbook vii

1. It Starts with You 1
- Transition Journal 2
- The Habit of Journaling 3
- Strengths and Weaknesses 3

2. What's Your Sign? 4
- Strengths 6
- Your Personal Brand Amplifier 7
- Values 7
- Your Values Worksheet 8
- Passions 9
- Purpose 10
- Personal Brand Amplifier 12
- Coaches 12

3. You've Accomplished a Lot! 13
- Making a List and Checking It Twice 13
- Who Do You Know? 27
- What Did You Do? 31
- Accomplishment Amplifier 32
- Memory Jogger: Let's Do Coffee 33
- Feedback 33
- Writing the Stories 34
- PAR Analysis Amplifier 35

4. It Begins and Ends with Your Network 36
- Types of Networks 36
- Evaluating Your Network 38
- Caution: Network Under Construction 38
- Your Network Amplifier 39
- Who's in Your Tribe? 41
- Mirror, Mirror, on the Wall 42

5. The Ins and Outs of Networking 44

6. Your Resume (It's About Time!) 46
- Resume Amplifier 46
- Resume Amplifier Worksheet 47
- How Many Resumes Do I Need? 49

7. Marketing—with a Twist 58
- Sales Funnels 58
- TAM, SAM, and SOM Decoded 59
- Amplify Your Job Search's Top Ten Lists 59
- SOM Amplifier Worksheet 60
- Time to Go to the Library 62
- From TAM to SAM 62
- Other Sources 63

8. Ready? Set? Go! 64
- Time Is on Your Side 64

Keeping Track of It All 64
SOM Amplifier Revisted 65
Hmmm...What's This Thread? 65
Preparation: The Difference between Winning and Losing 66
Connections 68
The Ask 70
No Connection 71

9. Let's Get Creative 72
Update Your Resume 73

10. The First Date and Beyond 79
Back to Social 79
Interviewer Prep Amplifier 79
Competition Prep Amplifier 79
Day in the Life Prep Amplifier 84
The Question 88
After the Interview 89
Thank-You Notes 90

11. The End Game 91
Success! You've Gotten the Offer 91
Lucky You! You Have Multiple Offers 91
Offer Evaluation Amplifier 92
You Got the Job! Your Dream Job! 93
Two Pledges 95

Bibliography 97

Extra Amplifiers and Worksheets 99
Your Personal Brand Amplifier 100
Accomplishment Amplifier 103
PAR Analysis Amplifier 105
Your Network Amplifier 110
Resume Amplifier Worksheet 112
SOM Amplifier Worksheet 114
Interview Prep Amplifier 116
Interviewer Prep Amplifier 121
Competition Prep Amplifier 131
Day in the Life Prep Amplifier 136
Offer Evaluation Amplifier 151

About the Author 157

How to Use This Workbook

You've been terminated. Laid off. RIFed. Fired.

Or, you are fed up. Burned out. Frustrated. Ready to quit.

If you are reading this workbook, chances are good you have read, or are reading, *Amplify Your Job Search: Strategies for Finding Your Dream Job*. If you don't have a copy, you will need to pick up a copy in either paperback, ebook, or audiobook format. This workbook is designed to complement that book; it is not a standalone workbook. If you don't have a copy, you can pick one up at www.JeffreySTon.com/author-amplify-your-job-search. While you are at it, pick up a copy of *Amplify Your Job Search: Transition Journal* at www.JeffreySTon.com/author-amplify-your-job-search-journal. You will then have all the tools you will need to start searching for your dream job!

All the Amplifiers from *Amplify Your Job Search* are here in one easy-to-access place. I've also included additional worksheets and tools to give you additional support as you navigate your search. This workbook is divided into chapters that align with the primary text. That means if you are reading chapter 3, "You've Accomplished a Lot!," you will be completing the work within the chapter of the same name here.

I suggest you skim through this workbook to familiarize yourself with it. Once you have finished, come right back here and prepare for chapter 1, "It Starts with You."

1

It Starts with You

Whether you are in transition or you are currently employed and have made the decision to look for employment elsewhere, it is an emotional time. A job change is one of life's most significant stressors.

Spend some time thinking about what you are feeling as you embark on this journey. Rate yourself on the scales by placing an X along the continuums.

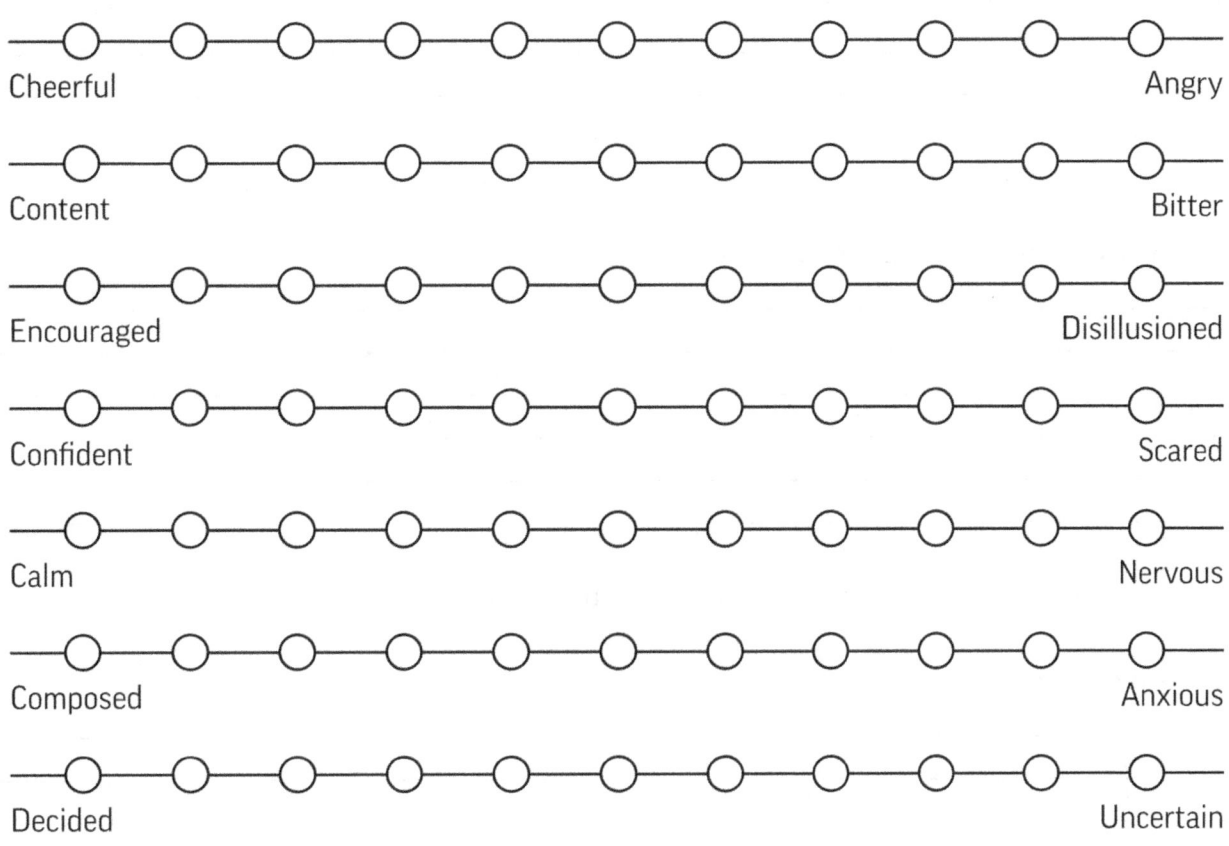

Cheerful ○ ○ ○ ○ ○ ○ ○ ○ ○ ○ ○ Angry

Content ○ ○ ○ ○ ○ ○ ○ ○ ○ ○ ○ Bitter

Encouraged ○ ○ ○ ○ ○ ○ ○ ○ ○ ○ ○ Disillusioned

Confident ○ ○ ○ ○ ○ ○ ○ ○ ○ ○ ○ Scared

Calm ○ ○ ○ ○ ○ ○ ○ ○ ○ ○ ○ Nervous

Composed ○ ○ ○ ○ ○ ○ ○ ○ ○ ○ ○ Anxious

Decided ○ ○ ○ ○ ○ ○ ○ ○ ○ ○ ○ Uncertain

The nature of stress is that it compounds. The more of life's events we are navigating at the same time, the more stress we are likely to feel. In addition to your job search, what else is going on in your life now? Some examples might include change in marital status, birth of a child, loss of a parent, illness or injury to yourself, and illness or injury to someone you love.

What other life events are you experiencing?

Transition Journal

Do you already keep a journal? ________

What types of journals do you keep?

What benefits do you receive from journaling?

If you don't keep a journal today, have you journaled in the past? ________

If so, why did you stop?

The Habit of Journaling

How often, when, and where you journal are important aspects of forming the habit of journaling.

How often will you commit to journaling?

___

When will you journal?

___

Where will you journal?

___

Strengths and Weaknesses

List ten of your strengths:

___
___
___
___
___
___
___
___
___
___

List ten of your weaknesses:

___
___
___
___
___
___
___
___
___
___

Review your list of weaknesses. Cross out the weaknesses that you could rely on others to complement. Be sure to read this section of *Amplify Your Job Search* to guide you in determining which weaknesses to cross out.

2

What's Your Sign?

Before completing the exercises in chapter 2, write a description of your personal brand:

Have you tried to carefully cultivate your brand, or has it been unintentional? Indicate where you fall on the spectrum with an X.

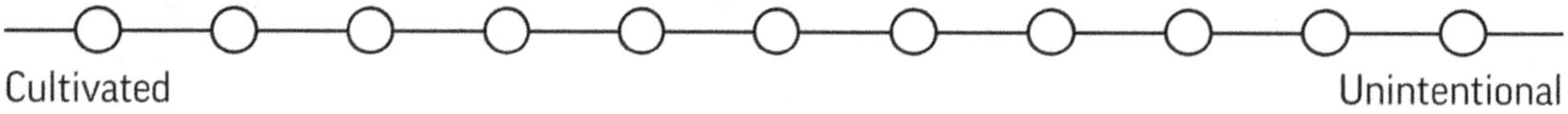

Call a friend, someone you trust to give honest feedback. Have them look you up on LinkedIn. Ask them to describe you based on what they see. What impression do they have based solely on your LinkedIn profile?

Call another friend and have them look you up on Facebook. What impression do they have based solely on your Facebook profile and newsfeed?

Call yet another friend and have them look you up on Instagram. What impression do they have based solely on your Instagram posts?

Finally, call a fourth friend and have them find you on Twitter. What impression do they have based on your profile and your tweets?

Use your favorite internet search engine to search for yourself. How many entries on page 1 are about you? ________

What picture do the results paint of you and your personal brand?

Four components make up your personal brand: strengths, values, passions, and purpose. We will review each one using a three-step process. Step one is self-reflection. In this step you will answer a series of questions in your journal. Next, take an assessment that measures the component (if you are working with a coach, please follow their recommendations). In the third step, you will ask for feedback from people who know you.

On the next page, you will find the first of five tools, the Personal Brand Amplifier™. We will use the Personal Brand Amplifier and your Transition Journal to complete the remaining exercises in this chapter.

Strengths

The key here is to know and understand your strengths. The goal will be to list your top five strengths. You've done a little bit of this work in chapter 1.

Self-Reflection

After completing the self-reflection journaling exercise about your strengths, begin to fill in the Personal Brand Amplifier.

Around the dial you will notice major "clicks" and minor "clicks" representing amping up your brand. Each major click is labeled with one of the four components of your personal brand: strengths, values, passions, purpose.

Next to the minor clicks under "Strengths," write your top five strengths beside each click.

Assessment

After completing the strengths assessment and the readout, compare the results with the strengths you listed in your Personal Brand Amplifier.

What are the similarities?

____

____

____

____

What are the surprises?

____

____

____

____

Make any changes you feel compelled to make to your Personal Brand Amplifier. Be sure to write in your journal what changes you made and why.

YOUR PERSONAL BRAND AMPLIFIER

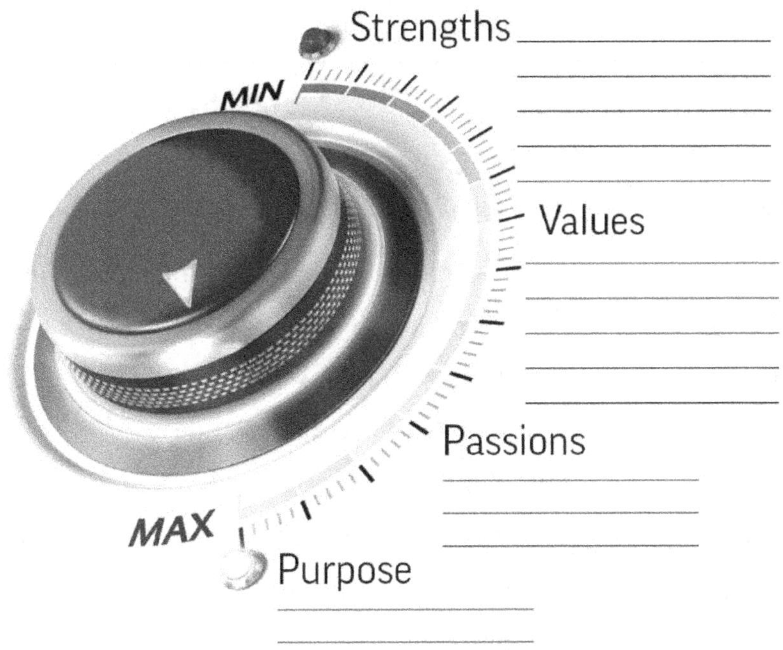

Feedback

After receiving the feedback from your network, return to this workbook. Compare the results with those in your Personal Brand Amplifier. Make any changes, and of course capture your reasons in your Transition Journal.

Values

We are now going to repeat that process of self-reflection, assessment, and feedback for your values.

Self-Reflection

On the next page is a list of values. Review the list and put a check by those that align with you. Cross out those that do not apply. Review the values with check marks. Identify the ones that are the most important to you by underlining them. Cross out the ones you did not underline. If you have more than five, identify the ones that are nonnegotiable. Cross out the others.

On your Personal Brand Amplifier, under the "Values" click, write your five values next to the minor clicks. Many times, the definition of a value word could be ambiguous (e.g., what I think is a challenge

YOUR VALUES WORKSHEET

Objective: Narrow this list to five values to which you relate the most.
Scan the list and highlight all the ones you identify with the most. Add any that may be missing. Then scratch off values that are not as important as others until you have five clearly defined.

Accessibility	Courage	Empathy	Calmness
Honesty	Originality	Speed	Love
Accomplishment	Creativity	Enthusiasm	Discipline
Humor	Passion	Spirituality	Sensitivity
Accountability	Curiosity	Excellence	Growth
Imagination	Peace	Spontaneity	Charity
Accuracy	Dependability	Experience	Optimism
Impact	Perfection	Stability	Control
Adventure	Determination	Expertise	Respect
Independence	Power	Strength	Directness
Affection	Clarity	Fairness	Security
Integrity	Prosperity	Success	Grace
Affluence	Comfort	Faith	Challenge
Intelligence	Punctuality	Sympathy	Mindfulness
Altruism	Commitment	Fame	Efficiency
Justice	Recognition	Teamwork	Sincerity
Ambition	Compassion	Family	Generosity
Kindness	Relaxation	Understanding	Celebrity
Assertiveness	Completion	Fidelity	Loyalty
Knowledge	Reliability	Vision	Diversity
Balance	Contentment	Flexibility	Significance
Leadership	Resourcefulness	Wealth	Health
Bravery	Control	Fun	Learning
	Respect	Winning	

might not be a challenge to you). For each value word you wrote on the Amplifier, in your journal, write one or two sentences that define the value for you (i.e., Challenge: I like assignments that challenge me mentally to solve a puzzle or learn something new).

Assessment

After completing the assessment and the readout, compare the results with the values you listed in your Personal Brand Amplifier.

What are the similarities?

____

____

____

____

What are the surprises?

____

____

____

____

Make any changes you feel compelled to make to your Personal Brand Amplifier. Be sure to write in your journal what changes you made and why.

Feedback

After receiving feedback about your values, compare the results with those in your Personal Brand Amplifier. Make any changes, and of course capture your reasons in your Transition Journal.

Passions

Let's talk about your passions. You know, things that are your jam! Things that get you jazzed up. Things that when you talk about them, your face lights up, your voice gets that added inflection, and your body language screams "I *love* this!" What are those things? Write them down (you knew that was coming by now, didn't you?).

____

____

____

____

____

____

____

Self-Reflection

Complete the Self-Reflection journaling exercise. The next major click of your Personal Brand Amplifier is passions. Next to the minor clicks under "Passions," add two or three of your passions.

Assessment

After completing the assessment and the readout, compare the results with the passions you listed in your Personal Brand Amplifier.

What are the similarities?

____

____

____

____

____

What are the surprises?

____

____

____

____

____

Make any changes you feel compelled to make to your Personal Brand Amplifier. Be sure to write in your journal what changes you made and why.

Feedback

After receiving the feedback about your passions, compare the results with those in your Personal Brand Amplifier. Make any changes, and of course capture your reasons in your Transition Journal.

Purpose

The final step into understanding your personal brand is to identify your purpose. (Haven't you always wanted to know your purpose in life, anyway?) But what is a purpose anyway? The Oxford dictionary defines purpose as "the reason for which something is done or created or for which something exists". John Qualls, CEO of Purpose HQ, defines purpose this way: "Your purpose is using your talent and skills to solve a problem people care about and need the solution, and you are rewarded for it."

Self-Reflection

Complete the Self-Reflection journaling activity to help you clarify your purpose.

Read over what you have written.

Which of the problems that you solved related to your passions?

Which ones aligned with your values?

Which ones used the most of your strengths?

Pick one. On your Personal Brand Amplifier, on the minor clicks under "Purpose," list no more than two purposes you identified next to the clicks under Purpose.

Assessment

After completing the assessment and the readout, compare the results with the purpose you listed on your Personal Brand Amplifier.

What are the similarities?

What are the surprises?

____
____
____
____
____

Make any changes you feel compelled to make to your Personal Brand Amplifier. Be sure to write in your journal what changes you made and why.

Feedback

When you have received all the feedback regarding your Personal Brand Amplifier, compare the results with those in your Personal Brand Amplifier. Make any changes, and of course capture your reasons in your Transition Journal.

Personal Brand Amplifier

Make a copy of the page with your Personal Brand Amplifier. Hang it someplace where you will see it every day.

Coaches

Did you decide to hire a coach to guide you on this journey? Write their name and contact information here.

Name: ______________________________

Address: ______________________________

____

Phone: ______________________________

If you have had an initial consultation with them, write a recap of the session and what things they advise you to work on for the next few weeks.

____
____
____
____
____
____
____
____
____
____
____
____

3

You've Accomplished a Lot!

You've done a lot in your career. You've learned some great lessons. You've accomplished some great things. Can you remember them all? Now is the time to try! n this chapter you will build a list of your accomplishments, refine that list, and begin to prepare a subset of the list for your—you guessed it—resume!

Making a List and Checking It Twice

What year did you graduate from high school? ________

What was the name of the school, and where was it located?

____

____

Did you have a summer job between graduation and college? Where did you work?

____

____

____

____

____

____

When did you work there?

Start: ______________________

End: ______________________

Where did you go to college?

____

____

____

When did you attend?

Start: ______________

End: ______________

List the organizations you were associated with during those years: fraternity, sorority, campus organizations, church organizations, clubs you belonged, and summer jobs, internships, jobs during the academic year.

____

____

____

____

____

____

____

Did you serve in the military? ________

What branch? ______________

When did you serve?

Start: ______________

End: ______________

Where did you serve?

____

____

____

____

____

____

What ranks did you hold?

What specialized training did you receive?

Did you receive any special commendations?

Did you pursue any advanced degrees? ________

What school(s) did you attend?

When did you attend?

Start: ______________________

End: ______________________

What degree(s) did you earn?

Now let's look at your full-time employment.

Job 1

What was your first full-time job? ______________________________

Where did you work? ______________________________

When did you work there?

Start: ______________________________

End: ______________________________

What roles or titles did you hold while there?

____
____
____
____
____
____
____

List all the organizations you were associated with while you worked there (volunteer organizations, side jobs, church organizations, board positions):

____
____
____
____
____
____
____
____
____
____
____
____
____

Job 2

What was your next job? ______________________________

Where did you work? ______________________________

When did you work there?

Start: ______________

End: ______________

What roles or titles did you hold while there?

____
____
____
____
____
____
____

List all the organizations you were associated with while you worked there (volunteer organizations, side jobs, church organizations, board positions):

____
____
____
____
____
____
____
____
____
____
____
____
____

Job 3

What was your next job? ______________________________

Where did you work? ______________________________

When did you work there?

Start: ______________

End: ______________

What roles or titles did you hold while there?

____
____
____
____
____
____
____

List all the organizations you were associated with while you worked there (volunteer organizations, side jobs, church organizations, board positions):

____
____
____
____
____
____
____
____
____
____
____
____
____

Job 4

What was your next job? ______________________________

Where did you work? ______________________________

When did you work there?

Start: ____________________

End: ____________________

What roles or titles did you hold while there?

____
____
____
____
____
____
____

List all the organizations you were associated with while you worked there (volunteer organizations, side jobs, church organizations, board positions):

____
____
____
____
____
____
____
____
____
____
____
____
____

Job 5

What was your next job? ______________________________

Where did you work? ______________________________

When did you work there?

Start: ____________________

End: ____________________

What roles or titles did you hold while there?

List all the organizations you were associated with while you worked there (volunteer organizations, side jobs, church organizations, board positions):

Job 6

What was your next job? ____________________

Where did you work? ____________________

When did you work there?

Start: ____________________

End: ____________________

What roles or titles did you hold while there?

____
____
____
____
____
____
____

List all the organizations you were associated with while you worked there (volunteer organizations, side jobs, church organizations, board positions):

____
____
____
____
____
____
____
____
____
____
____
____
____

Job 7

What was your next job? ______________________________

Where did you work? ______________________________

When did you work there?

Start: ______________

End: ______________

What roles or titles did you hold while there?

____
____
____
____
____
____
____

List all the organizations you were associated with while you worked there (volunteer organizations, side jobs, church organizations, board positions):

____
____
____
____
____
____
____
____
____
____
____
____
____

Job 8

What was your next job? ______________________________

Where did you work? ______________________________

When did you work there?

Start: ____________________

End: ____________________

What roles or titles did you hold while there?

List all the organizations you were associated with while you worked there (volunteer organizations, side jobs, church organizations, board positions):

Job 9

What was your next job? ______________________________

Where did you work? ______________________________

When did you work there?

Start: ______________

End: ______________

What roles or titles did you hold while there?

____
____
____
____
____
____
____

List all the organizations you were associated with while you worked there (volunteer organizations, side jobs, church organizations, board positions):

____
____
____
____
____
____
____
____
____
____
____
____
____

Job 10

What was your next job? ______________________________

Where did you work? ______________________________

When did you work there?

Start: ______________

End: ______________

What roles or titles did you hold while there?

____
____
____
____
____
____
____

List all the organizations you were associated with while you worked there (volunteer organizations, side jobs, church organizations, board positions):

____
____
____
____
____
____
____
____
____
____
____
____
____

Did you experience any gaps in your employment history longer than one month? ________

Write a description of one of the gaps:

When did the gap start and end?

Start: ____________________________

End: ____________________________

List the organizations you were involved with during this time:

Who Do You Know?

Go back through the list. Write down the names of as many people in those organizations you can remember. Who was that kid you hung out with in college? What were the names of your superiors in the service? Who were your bosses, your coworkers? If you were a den mother for Cub Scouts, what were the names of the other adults? If you sat on a board for your church, who else was on that board?

I remember:

______________ from my time at ______________

______________ from my time at ______________

______________ from my time at ______________

______________ from my time at ______________

______________ from my time at ______________

______________ from my time at ______________

______________ from my time at ______________

______________ from my time at ______________

______________ from my time at ______________

______________ from my time at ______________

______________ from my time at ______________

______________ from my time at ______________

______________ from my time at ______________

______________ from my time at ______________

______________ from my time at ______________

______________ from my time at ______________

______________ from my time at ______________

______________ from my time at ______________

______________ from my time at ______________

______________ from my time at ______________

______________ from my time at ______________

______________ from my time at ______________

______________ from my time at ______________

______________ from my time at ______________

______________ from my time at ______________

______________ from my time at ______________

______________ from my time at ______________

______________ from my time at ______________

______________ from my time at ______________

______________ from my time at ______________

______________ from my time at ______________

______________ from my time at ______________

_______________ from my time at _______________

_______________ from my time at _______________

_______________ from my time at _______________

_______________ from my time at _______________

_______________ from my time at _______________

_______________ from my time at _______________

_______________ from my time at _______________

_______________ from my time at _______________

_______________ from my time at _______________

_______________ from my time at _______________

_______________ from my time at _______________

_______________ from my time at _______________

_______________ from my time at _______________

_______________ from my time at _______________

_______________ from my time at _______________

_______________ from my time at _______________

_______________ from my time at _______________

_______________ from my time at _______________

_______________ from my time at _______________

_______________ from my time at _______________

_______________ from my time at _______________

_______________ from my time at _______________

_______________ from my time at _______________

_______________ from my time at _______________

_______________ from my time at _______________

_______________ from my time at _______________

_______________ from my time at _______________

_______________ from my time at _______________

_______________ from my time at _______________

_______________ from my time at _______________

_______________ from my time at _______________

_______________ from my time at _______________

_______________ from my time at _______________

_______________ from my time at _______________

_______________ from my time at _______________

_______________ from my time at _______________

_______________ from my time at _______________

_______________ from my time at _______________

_______________ from my time at _______________

_______________ from my time at _______________

____________________ from my time at ____________________
____________________ from my time at ____________________
____________________ from my time at ____________________
____________________ from my time at ____________________
____________________ from my time at ____________________
____________________ from my time at ____________________
____________________ from my time at ____________________
____________________ from my time at ____________________
____________________ from my time at ____________________
____________________ from my time at ____________________
____________________ from my time at ____________________
____________________ from my time at ____________________
____________________ from my time at ____________________
____________________ from my time at ____________________
____________________ from my time at ____________________
____________________ from my time at ____________________
____________________ from my time at ____________________
____________________ from my time at ____________________
____________________ from my time at ____________________
____________________ from my time at ____________________
____________________ from my time at ____________________
____________________ from my time at ____________________
____________________ from my time at ____________________
____________________ from my time at ____________________
____________________ from my time at ____________________
____________________ from my time at ____________________
____________________ from my time at ____________________
____________________ from my time at ____________________
____________________ from my time at ____________________
____________________ from my time at ____________________
____________________ from my time at ____________________
____________________ from my time at ____________________
____________________ from my time at ____________________
____________________ from my time at ____________________
____________________ from my time at ____________________
____________________ from my time at ____________________
____________________ from my time at ____________________
____________________ from my time at ____________________
____________________ from my time at ____________________
____________________ from my time at ____________________

____________________ from my time at ____________________
____________________ from my time at ____________________
____________________ from my time at ____________________
____________________ from my time at ____________________
____________________ from my time at ____________________
____________________ from my time at ____________________
____________________ from my time at ____________________
____________________ from my time at ____________________
____________________ from my time at ____________________
____________________ from my time at ____________________
____________________ from my time at ____________________
____________________ from my time at ____________________
____________________ from my time at ____________________
____________________ from my time at ____________________
____________________ from my time at ____________________
____________________ from my time at ____________________
____________________ from my time at ____________________
____________________ from my time at ____________________
____________________ from my time at ____________________
____________________ from my time at ____________________
____________________ from my time at ____________________
____________________ from my time at ____________________
____________________ from my time at ____________________
____________________ from my time at ____________________
____________________ from my time at ____________________
____________________ from my time at ____________________
____________________ from my time at ____________________
____________________ from my time at ____________________
____________________ from my time at ____________________
____________________ from my time at ____________________
____________________ from my time at ____________________
____________________ from my time at ____________________
____________________ from my time at ____________________
____________________ from my time at ____________________
____________________ from my time at ____________________
____________________ from my time at ____________________
____________________ from my time at ____________________
____________________ from my time at ____________________
____________________ from my time at ____________________
____________________ from my time at ____________________

__________ from my time at __________
__________ from my time at __________
__________ from my time at __________
__________ from my time at __________
__________ from my time at __________
__________ from my time at __________
__________ from my time at __________
__________ from my time at __________
__________ from my time at __________
__________ from my time at __________
__________ from my time at __________
__________ from my time at __________
__________ from my time at __________
__________ from my time at __________
__________ from my time at __________
__________ from my time at __________
__________ from my time at __________
__________ from my time at __________
__________ from my time at __________
__________ from my time at __________
__________ from my time at __________
__________ from my time at __________
__________ from my time at __________
__________ from my time at __________
__________ from my time at __________
__________ from my time at __________
__________ from my time at __________
__________ from my time at __________
__________ from my time at __________
__________ from my time at __________
__________ from my time at __________
__________ from my time at __________

Mark the ones you are friends with on Facebook with an F.
Mark the people you are connected with on LinkedIn with an L.
Indicate those you follow on Instagram with an I and those you follow on Twitter with a T.

What Did You Do?

Transfer your career timeline from your transition journal to the Accomplishment Amplifier™ on the next page. Try to keep the jobs in chronological order as best you can. Use the "Start Date" to maintain the order.

ACCOMPLISHMENT AMPLIFIER

START DATE	END DATE	COMPANY / ORGANIZATION	ROLE/TITLE	RESPONSIBILITIES	ACCOMPLISHMENTS	PROBLEM	ACTION	RESULTS

Once you have your list transferred, start at the first row. Under the Responsibilities column, add a few sentences or bullet points to describe the responsibilities you had while in that role. Be as specific as you can, but if you can't remember all the details, that is okay. You will be coming back to this list, and you can add more details as you recall them.

As you are filling in the responsibilities, if an accomplishment occurs to you, go ahead and add that under the Accomplishments column. Don't focus on trying to fill out both responsibilities and accomplishments, just capture them as they occur to you.

Now that you have responsibilities for each role, start back at the top and add accomplishments under that column. Try to list at least three for each role. It's okay to use bullet points. Be as detailed as you can; however, if the details are a bit fuzzy, you can add them later.

Memory Jogger: Let's Do Coffee

If you are like me, you will need a memory jogger (or two, or three). If you have some gaps in your Accomplishment Amplifier, reach out to one or two of your connections from that time period. Invite them to coffee (or tea, lunch, beer, a phone call, or a Zoom call).

List the people you are meeting:

____

____

____

____

____

____

Go back to your Accomplishment Amplifier and fill in the details from your notes. Have as many coffee meetings as it takes to have at least three accomplishments for every role.

Feedback

Time for more coffee! Now is the time to share your Accomplishment Amplifier. Share it with your coach, a mentor, your spouse, a friend, or all of the above. Invite them to coffee. Review the list with them. Invite them to ask questions.

Who is reviewing your Accomplishment Amplifier?

____

____

____

____

____

Which accomplishments did they ask about? Mark them on your Accomplishment Amplifier.

What questions did they ask?

Between these coffee meetings, review your Accomplishment Amplifier. Add notes and details from your conversations. Refer to your Personal Brand Amplifier. Do the accomplishments underscore your strengths, values, passions, and purpose? Which of your stories were more compelling? Why? Did they align more with your Personal Brand Amplifier? Did you learn something through this process that compels you to modify the Personal Brand Amplifier? Update it. It's okay; it's *your* personal brand!

Writing the Stories

Now it's time to hone your stories and have some more coffee. Take your Accomplishment Amplifier and meet with a few more people from your network or, perhaps even better, new additions to your network. Share the Accomplishment Amplifier with them and tell your stories. Take notes and be sure to update your Accomplishment Amplifier and your Personal Brand Amplifier.

Who is reviewing your Accomplishment Amplifier?

Which accomplishments did they ask about? Mark them on your Accomplishment Amplifier.

What questions did they ask?

PAR ANALYSIS AMPLIFIER

PROBLEM:
ACTIONS:
RESULTS:
RESUME BULLET:
SKILLS USED:

4

It Begins and Ends with Your Network

As you may have surmised by now, I am a big proponent of networking. (For you information technology pros out there, I am not talking about the kind of networking that connects computer systems together; I am talking about the kind of networking that connects people together.) At the time of this writing, 87 percent of jobs are filled through your network (up from 43 percent ten years ago). The old adage "It's not what you know but who you know" rings truer and truer. But this is not about nepotism. This is about the value of a warm introduction that separates you from hundreds of other job seekers.

How many connections do you have on LinkedIn? ________

I had twenty when I started my job transition ten years ago.

Types of Networks

Now that you get the why of networking, let's talk about the types of networking, and then we will get into the how. There are four primary types of networking opportunities. Over the course of this chapter we will explore how to leverage each one to help you land that perfect job.

Professional Networking Events

How many professional network events have you attended in the last year (include virtual events that allowed attendee to attendee communication)? ________

Networking Groups

Do you belong to any professional networking groups? List them:

____

____

____

Have you joined any job seeker networking groups? List them:

Community Networks

What community groups are you involved with? Include church, civic, or other groups. List them:

One-on-One Networking

Review the lists you made in the previous sections. List at least one person from each group you could contact for a one-on-one networking meeting (face-to-face or virtual):

Social Networks

What social media networks do you use (e.g., Facebook, LinkedIn, etc.)? List them:

____

____

____

____

____

____

Evaluating Your Network

Network Amplifier

The Network Amplifier™ is made up of spokes (the lines) and nodes (the circles). Take some time now to fill out your Network Amplifier.

In the center node, write your name. Think of all the events you have attended in the last year. Write those events in the nodes connected to "Events & Conferences." Add more spokes and nodes if needed.

Proceed to the "Networking Groups" node. How many professional or industry groups are you currently involved with? Off the "Professional" node, write the names of those groups. Have you joined a job seekers group? Fill in those nodes, as well. Add more spokes and more nodes if needed.

Next up, think of the community groups you are involved with. Write those groups off the appropriate nodes. Add additional spokes and nodes to represent all your community groups.

Finally, for the "One-on-One" node, fill in the names of everyone you know. I'm kidding! To complete this portion of the Amplifier, we will use numbers to represent your network. In the "Family" node, write the number of family members with whom you have spoken with in the last year. In the "Friends" node, write the number of friends you have seen or spoken with in the last six months. In the nodes that represent your social media connections, write the number of connections, friends, or followers you have in each. Add more spokes and nodes if you need.

Review your Network Amplifier. In your Transition Journal, reflect on your connections. Do you have a lot (by your definition)? Are there obvious gaps? What does this tell you about your level of connectedness? How does it make you feel?

Caution: Network Under Construction

Before turning our attention to the nuts and bolts of how to network, let's spend some time on building your network. Go back to your Network Amplifier. Where were the gaps? If you haven't attended more than one or two professional networking events in the last year, start by identifying the ones in your area. Use the search engine of your choice to find some. Talk to your peers and find out which ones they attend. Read the business section of your local paper or your local business journal. Are there trade associations for your industry or your profession? Locate their websites and look for conferences.

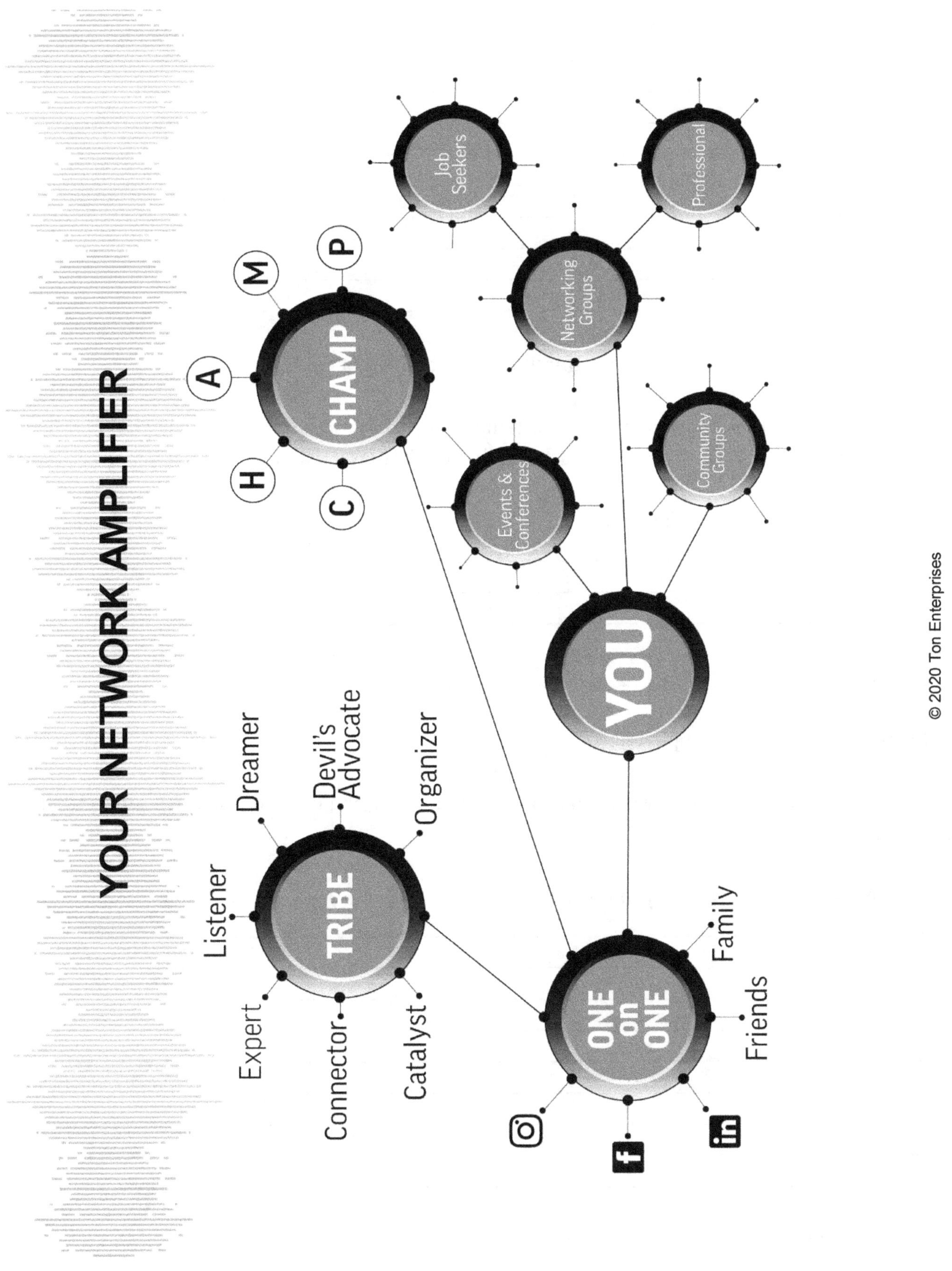
YOUR NETWORK AMPLIFIER
CHAMP
C
H
A
M
P
Job Seekers
Professional
Networking Groups
Events & Conferences
Community Groups
YOU
TRIBE
Listener
Dreamer
Devil's Advocate
Organizer
Expert
Connector
Catalyst
ONE on ONE
Family
Friends
© 2020 Ton Enterprises

List the networking events you find here:

Add the ones you listed to your Network Amplifier using a different color.

Repeat this process with networking groups, both industry and job seekers groups. Ask your coach for recommendations. Reach out to peers, and ask which ones they attend and why.

List the networking groups you find here:

Add them to your Network Amplifier.

Lather, rinse, repeat for community organizations. Have a hobby or a passion? Research groups that meet to talk about it.

List the community organizations you find here:

Update your Network Amplifier.

Who's in Your Tribe?

Jason Barnaby, founder of Fire Starters, Inc., and the author of *Igniting the Fire Starter Within: The Secrets to Finding Your Fire, Fanning Your Flame, and Tending Your Tribe*, has developed a great resource for identifying the different types of people you need in your network. His Tribal Inventory describes seven quintessential roles members everyone should have in their tribe.

- **Listener:** Unsurprisingly, this is the person who listens. They provide an ear for your ideas, ramblings, and plans. They ask questions and they rarely, if ever, offer advice.
- **Dreamer:** Their favorite phrase is "what if." They take your ideas and give you dozens of ideas to build upon. The bigger the ideas, the better!
- **Devil's Advocate:** They burst bubbles. They poke holes in your dreams and your big ideas. Sounds bad, right? It's not! They serve a critical role in keeping us grounded and real. They allow us to add detail to our dreams.
- **Organizer:** This is the list maker. They help you think through the "this before that" steps you need to take to make your dream a reality.
- **Catalyst:** They give you a kick in the seat of the pants when you need one. They encourage you, they challenge you, and they hold you accountable. They give you the push you need to create the best version of you.
- **Connector:** A connector's favorite phrases are "You need to meet so and so" and "You need to read this book or blog post." They love making introductions for the sake of watching the network grow. They are the lines on your Network Amplifier.
- **Expert:** They are your guide because they've already been there. They can provide directions and insights. They won't necessarily tell you how to navigate every bend in the river, but they will be there with advice along the journey.

On your Network Amplifier, find the Tribe node—it's near the One-on-One node you completed earlier. Write the names of the person or people who serve in each of the seven roles your Tribal Inventory.

What is your role in others' tribes? List the person and the role you play:

Mirror, Mirror, on the Wall

When you think of the people in your network, what do they look like? I mean it literally: What do they look like? Do they all look the same? Do they all share a similar background, a similar belief system?

Write your perception of the diversity of your network:

To begin, think about your network in terms of the acronym CHAMP. CHAMP stands for customer, hire, associate, mentor, protege. Locate the CHAMP node on your Network Amplifier.

By the C node, write the name of someone in your network who is your customer (current, past, or prospective). This is not someone who works for the same company as you.

H stands for hire. Write the name of someone you would recommend a friend hire, someone who you would stake your reputation on.

Associate is the A in CHAMP. List the name of a person in your previous (or current) organization who holds a similar role as you. If you were a vice president, this would be another vice president.

Mentors are a valuable part of your network. Do you have a mentor? Write down their name. Don't have one? This is a gap you will want to fill!

P is for protege, someone you mentor. You do mentor someone, don't you? You can learn more from mentoring someone than just about any other type of networking.

In your Transition Journal, reflect on your CHAMP network. Are there gaps? Is there someone that comes to mind who could fill the gap? Are there other names you could add?

Go ahead and write them on your Network Amplifier in a different color.

In this next part, we are going to dig a little deeper. We are going to see how diverse your network is today. To do this, we are going to use the CHAMP node again.

The I in IGGNORE is for industry. Look at your CHAMP nodes. Write an I next to the names of anyone who is in a different industry than the one in which you work (or most recently worked).

The first G is for generation. We live and work at a time when there are as many as five generations in the workforce. For our purposes, let's focus on four: baby boomers (born 1946–1964), generation X (born 1965–1980), millennials (born 1981–1996), and generation Z (born 1997–2012). Write a G next to anyone in your CHAMP nodes that are in a different generation than you are in.

Next up is gender. Gender and gender identity can be a complex subject for those who have not been introduced appropriately to the topic. Amy Waninger does a masterful job in the chapter on gender identity in her book. For our purposes, we will use male, female, nonbinary (a gender identity that is neither male nor female), and transgender (a person whose gender identity differs from the gender they were assigned at birth). Think about your CHAMP nodes. Write GN next to anyone whose gender is different than your own.

The O in our exercise stands for orientation—sexual orientation. Straight, lesbian, gay, bisexual, queer, and so on. Review the names in your CHAMP network. Put an O next to the name of anyone whose orientation you know is different than your own.

The R stands for race and ethnicity. Again, focusing on your CHAMP network, do you have someone in your network who is of a different race or ethnicity from yours? Put an R next to their name.

The E in Amy's model stands for exchange—in other words, the depth of your relationship. Put an E next to anyone's name with whom you have exchanged personal stories or know them deeply, by your own definition.

Are there any letters you were not able to write down? Think about your Tribe network. Do any of those people fill the gaps in your IGGNORE exercise? Do you still have gaps? Think about the other One-on-One nodes: family, friends, etc. Does someone come to mind that represents the missing letters in your network?

List them here:

Write their names on your Network Amplifier along with the corresponding letter.

5

The Ins and Outs of Networking

In *Amplify Your Job Search,* chapter 5 provides you with several tips and best practices for upping your networking game. As a complement to that chapter, spend a few minutes in your workbook.

Describe how you typically feel in a room where the structure is to network with others:

When meeting someone you don't know or don't know well one-on-one, how do you feel?

This chapter provides several tips and tricks to help you network effectively. Which ones stood out to you?

After you have had a chance to try some of the suggestions, complete this section.

Which suggestions did you try? What were the results? What would you do differently next time?

6

Your Resume (It's About Time!)

Resume Amplifier

You will find extra copies of the Resume Amplifier™ at the back of this workbook. If you need more, make some copies. Of course, you can always download more from www.JeffreySTon.com/AYJS/Resources.

If you have several types of jobs in mind, you will want to complete a Resume Amplifier for each one. Simply repeat this process for completing each one.

Search the internet for the type of job you have in mind. Don't limit yourself to a specific job title, location, or company. For this process, those things aren't important. These may or may not be positions for which you apply. For now, focus on the jobs in which you can excel and that align with your Personal Brand Amplifier and your Accomplishment Amplifier. Collect five or six examples.

In the Title section of your Resume Amplifier, write each one of the titles from your sample job descriptions. Congratulations! These are actual jobs for which you qualify and have interest in performing. Review the titles. Are there commonalities? Are the same words used in multiple titles? Is there a title that is most common? From these titles write a title of your own that encompasses the commonalities. This will be your target job description.

Turn your attention to skills. Review each of your sample job descriptions. In the Skills section of your Resume Amplifier, list all the skills that appear in all the sample jobs. Next, list all the skills that appear in all but one of the sample jobs, then the skills that are listed in all but two, all but three, and so on. Repeat until you are listing skills that only appear in one. You know now the skills employers need to solve the problems they are facing. Next to each skill, self-rank your competency in those skills on a scale of zero to five, zero being a true gap between the required skills and your skills, and five meaning you are a true rock star in that area.

RESUME AMPLIFIER WORKSHEET

TITLE
Target Job Description

SKILLS	
Skill	**Rank (0-5)**

Rank 0 = True Gap 5 = Rock Star

RESPONSIBILITIES		
Responsibility	**Yrs.**	**Desire (1-5)**

EXPERIENCES		
Experience	**Yrs.**	**# Acc.**

DELIVERABLES		
Deliverable	**Deliver**	**Sample**
	Y / N	Y / N
	Y / N	Y / N
	Y / N	Y / N
	Y / N	Y / N
	Y / N	Y / N
	Y / N	Y / N
	Y / N	Y / N
	Y / N	Y / N
	Y / N	Y / N
	Y / N	Y / N

Now, let's focus on responsibilities. In the Responsibilities section of your Resume Amplifier, list the responsibilities that appear in all the sample jobs. Repeat the process described above to complete this section. When you've completed listing the responsibilities, rank both your experience in holding that responsibility and your desire to hold that responsibility. Your experience should be in number of years. Your desire should be on a scale of one to five. One being "Ugh, that is not something I would like to do" and five being "Heck yeah, rock on!"

Repeat this process for the Experience section of your Resume Amplifier. After completing the list, rank your experience in both your years of experience and your accomplishments related to that experience. Accomplishments is the number of accomplishments listed in your Accomplishment Amplifier related to that experience or similar experience.

Finally, your sample job descriptions may list specific deliverables you would be required to produce in this role. To complete your Resume Amplifier, repeat the review process. When your list is complete identify the deliverables with a yes or no. Yes, you have created such a deliverable in the past, or no, you have not. For each yes answer, add Y or N for each deliverable in your portfolio. Yes, you have a sample of that deliverable, or no, you do not.

In your Transition Journal, review the Resume Amplifier. Write down each of your target job titles. Answer the following questions:

I do or do not have the skill required to perform this job. ________

To excel at this job, I need to further develop my skills in:

____

____

This job has responsibilities I love to do. They are:

____

____

This job has some responsibilities I don't care for. They are:

____

____

For the latter, I would do these things to mitigate or compensate:

____

____

My experience aligns well with the experience required. To tell that story, I will highlight these accomplishments:

____

____

My portfolio of deliverables is robust, but I do have some gaps. I will work to fill those gaps by:

How Many Resumes Do I Need?

LinkedIn

In addition to a professional headshot, the Intro section should contain a headline that is more than just a repeat of your recent title. It's a headline. Use it to sell your personal brand.

Write your new LinkedIn headline:

Reference your Accomplishment Amplifier. Which ones are you most proud of and why?

Which ones speak to the story of your career?

Write your new LinkedIn About section:

Bio Resume

Your bio resume is very similar to the About section of your LinkedIn profile. It tells people who you are in a few paragraphs and maybe a handful of bullet points. It is less detailed than a full resume. If you have ever spoken at a conference or been on a panel, this is your introduction. In fact, once you have a bio resume, you can use it repeatedly for conferences.

Write your new bio here (it should be no fewer than fifty words and no longer than three hundred words):

General Resume

One of the things I point out in *Amplify Your Job Search* is the importance of the email address you provide to prospective employers with your resume. It should represent you and your brand. If yours does not, you will want to register for a new email address. Many people opt for something simple, like FirstName.LastName@emailprovider.com.

Write the email address you will be using on your resumes:

Write the contact section of your resume:

Write your target job title from your Resume Amplifier:

The performance profile is an important part of your resume, perhaps the most important part. Write a draft of your performance profile here:

List your professional skills/qualifications:

Refer to your PARs from chapter 3 and the resume bullets. Which ones tell your story? You will want to include those in the work experience section. List them here:

Have you had a gap in your work history? Write the story explaining the gap:

If you have had frequent job changes, write your story describing why:

List your education experience:

Have you ever roped a steer? No? What other additional experience tells the story of who you are and what your brand is?

Skills Inventory Addendum

Add as many of the skills you have developed throughout your career that you can list. Consider listing some more than once using acronyms and synonyms as described in *Amplify Your Job Search.*

Tailored Resume

What is the target job title of the position for which you are applying?

____

What are the keywords in the job description you need to use in your tailored resume?

______	______	______
______	______	______
______	______	______
______	______	______

What attributes should receive emphasis in the work experience section?

______	______	______
______	______	______
______	______	______

Are there specific skills you need to add to your resume?

______	______	______
______	______	______
______	______	______

7

Marketing—with a Twist

SALES FUNNELS

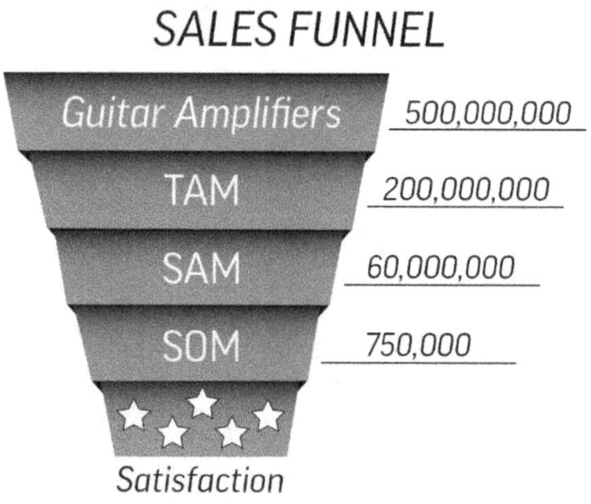

TAM, SAM, and SOM Decoded

- **Total Addressable Market (TAM)** is defined as the total market demand for a product or service.
- **Serviceable Addressable Market (SAM)** is defined as the portion of the TAM targeted and serviced by a company's product or service.
- **Share of Market (SOM)** is defined as the portion of the SAM that can realistically be reached.

How many companies in the world have jobs that align with your skills and passions? Make a wild guess: ________

How many companies in the geographic area where you would like to work have jobs that align with your skills and passions? Make another guess: ________

Amplify Your Job Search's Top Ten Lists

The next tool in our tool belt is the SOM Amplifier™. Its job is to help you narrow down the hundreds of thousand businesses and jobs to a much more manageable list. The first section of the SOM Amplifier is Amplify Your Job Search's Top Ten Lists.

Make a list of the top ten things you are looking for in your next position. Use your Personal Brand Amplifier, Accomplishment Amplifier, Network Amplifier, and Resume Amplifier to aid you in compiling the list. It's okay if you list more than ten.

Finished with the list? Good. Now force rank them 1 to 10, no ties. 1 is the most important thing you are looking for in your next job and 10 is the least important of your top ten. Write the ranked list in the Next Position section of your SOM Amplifier on the next page.

SOM AMPLIFIER WORKSHEET

AMPLIFY YOUR JOB SEARCH • TOP TEN LISTS

NEXT POSITION	SCORE
☐	
☐	
☐	
☐	
☐	
☐	
☐	
☐	
☐	
☐	

NEXT BOSS	SCORE
☐	
☐	
☐	
☐	
☐	
☐	
☐	
☐	
☐	
☐	

NEXT COMPANY	SCORE
☐	
☐	
☐	
☐	
☐	
☐	
☐	
☐	
☐	
☐	

Each Top 10 List scores a max of 55 points.

SEARCH CRITERIA		
FIELD	OPERATOR	VALUE

Next, repeat the process by creating a list of the top ten things you are looking for in your next boss:

Then list the top ten things you are looking for in your next company:

Force rank each of those lists, and then copy them to the corresponding section of your SOM Amplifier.

Before moving on to the next step, go back to your Resume Amplifier.

How many of the skills and responsibilities listed there show up on your SOM Amplifier? ________

If there are significant differences, consider repeating the Resume Amplifier exercise and using your Next Position Top Ten List as your search criteria as you search for job descriptions.

Time to Go to the Library

Log in to the Mergent Intellect database and go to "Search," then "Advanced Search." Familiarize yourself with the search criteria available. List the search criteria available:

On your Next Company Top Ten List, flag the items in your list that are searchable within Mergent. Identify other search criteria that would be useful. Run some searches as practice. The goal is to use as many criteria from your Next Company Top Ten List in your searches as you can. Write the search criteria on your SOM Amplifier.

From TAM to SAM

A list of 2,000 companies is great, but hardly manageable. Your next task is to reduce the list to a more manageable number. Use the remainder of your Next Company Top Ten List to eliminate some of the companies (at least for now). List the criteria and assumptions you used to reduce the list:

Other Sources

List other sources you could use to fine-tune your SAM List™:

8

Ready? Set? Go!

Time Is on Your Side

How will you allocate your time?

Networking Related Activities: ____________

Review Job Boards and Company Websites: ____________

Newsletters and Newspapers: ____________

Other: ____________

Other: ____________

Other: ____________

Total: ____________

Keeping Track of It All

What tracking tool will you be using?

____

SOM Amplifier Revisited

What's the first company on your SAM List?

____

How many of its employees are on LinkedIn? ________

How many of those are you connected with? ________

Do any of the employees have a job with your target job title? Who?

____

____

____

____

Are you connected with them? ________

Are any of your connections connected with them?

____

____

____

____

____

____

Hmmm...What's This Thread?

As you network, revisit this section often. What new threads have you discovered?

____

____

____

____

____

____

____

____

____

____

____

____

What companies can you add to your SAM List as result?

Preparation: The Difference between Winning and Losing

Pick the top two or three companies from your SAM List:

What are their social media handles?

List other sources (website, Glassdoor, internet search):

What topics are they discussing?

What are others saying about them?

Not only should you research the companies on your SAM List, but you should perform the same level of research on anyone you are meeting as part of your networking activities. Use LinkedIn, Google, and social media. Use the information to get to know them. What are they posting? What are they liking? Use the information to jot down a few questions to ask them when you meet.

Connections

As you network, use that same level of diligence to research your connections.

Who do you know who is connected with one of the top five companies on your SAM List?

What are their social media handles?

List other sources (website, Glassdoor, internet search):

What topics are they discussing?

What are others saying about them?

How well do you know them?

Not Much at All ○ ○ ○ ○ ○ ○ ○ ○ ○ ○ ○ BFFs

How candid will they be?

Very Reserved ○ ○ ○ ○ ○ ○ ○ ○ ○ ○ ○ Open Book

How long have they been at the company? ________

How many people are they connected with at the company? ________

Where are they in the organization's hierarchy?

What does all this say about their level of influence at the company?

The Ask

After meeting with a network connection, answer the following questions (you *did* ask the two asks, right?).

What can you do for them? (Remember, if they didn't have a specific answer, spend some time thinking about what you can do for them.)

What introductions did they say they would be making on your behalf?

No Connection

Who are your second-degree connections at one of your target companies?

Don't have any first- or second-degree connections? List the employees you are going to reach out to at the company:

9

Let's Get Creative

After reading chapter 9 in *Amplify Your Job Search*, what creative ideas resonated with you?

What other ideas did the examples spark?

Send your creative ways to get your resume noticed to jeff.ton@tonenterprisesllc.com.

Update Your Resume

Think about the conversations you have been having about your dream job. What words are you using to describe it?

What words do the others in your network use?

Think about the research you have been doing on LinkedIn, Twitter, Facebook, and Instagram. What words are being used there to describe the types of roles you are seeking?

Who are the thought leaders in your industry?

What are they writing?

What words are they using?

What problems are they solving?

Who are the future-thinkers in your industry?

What words are they using?

Pull out your Resume Amplifier. Review the keywords. Are there any that are outdated?

Are there new words being used today?

Are there new problems being discussed today?

Now, pick up your Accomplishment Amplifier. Do any of your accomplishments speak better to those new requirements than the ones you have been using in your Resume Amplifier and your resumes?

Finally, in doing this review, are there new skills required for your dream job?

What skills did you list that you need to develop?

What is your training plan to obtain those skills?

10

The First Date and Beyond

Congratulations—you have an interview! This might be your dream job. Let's get prepared.

Every time you get a call or email for an interview, begin to fill out the Interview Prep Amplifier™ (there are more copies at the back of this workbook, or you can download the PDF at www.JeffreySTon.com/AYJS/Resources).

Back to Social

Create a stream in your social media aggregator (as a reminder, I use Hootsuite) using keywords to narrow in on the industry or sector the company operates within. Set up another stream for the company itself. You will want to capture both what the company is saying and what others are saying about the company. Finally, set up another stream to capture what the interviewers you will be meeting with are posting.

Spend some time each day reviewing the streams. Read the links. Take notes. Jot down questions. Learn. Study.

Interviewer Prep Amplifier

Do you know the names of those who will be interviewing you? Complete an Interviewer Prep Amplifier™ for each one. (There are more copies at the back of this workbook.)

Competition Prep Amplifier

Research the competition—the company's competition, not your competition. Set up a stream that captures what they are saying (and what others are saying about them). Review that stream every day. Follow the links. Read the content. Take notes. Jot questions.

Visit the competition's website. Compare it to your target company's website. Where are they similar? Where are they differentiated? Guess what? Take notes. Jot questions.

INTERVIEW PREP AMPLIFIER

What is the name of the company asking for the interview?

What are their social media handles?

LinkedIn: Facebook:

Twitter: Other:

Instagram:

List other online/print sources: ***(Website, Glassdoor, Indeed, Search...)***

What topics are they discussing?

What are others saying about them?

What questions does that spark?

INTERVIEWER PREP AMPLIFIER

Name of the Interviewer:
What are their social media handles?
LinkedIn: Twitter: Instagram: Facebook:
List other online/print sources: ***(Website, Glassdoor, Indeed, Search…)***
What topics are they discussing?
What are others saying about them?

INTERVIEWER PREP AMPLIFIER (continued)

How long have they been at the company?
How many people are they connected with at the company?
Where are they in the organization's hierarchy?
What does all of this say about their level of influence at the company?
What questions does your research spark?

COMPETITION PREP AMPLIFIER

(Complete a Competition Prep Amplifier for each Competitor)

What is the name of the company's competitor?	
What are their social media handles?	
LinkedIn:	Facebook:
Twitter:	Other:
Instagram:	
List other online/print sources: ***(Website, Glassdoor, Indeed, Search...)***	
What topics are they discussing?	
What are others saying about them?	
What questions does that spark?	

Day in the Life Prep Amplifier

Use LinkedIn to connect with people at similar companies in similar roles. Reach out and ask for a short phone call. Find out what a day in the life is like in that role for that company. Ask if they know the company you are targeting. What can they tell you about your future employer? Be sure to take notes and jot down questions that come to mind.

Complete a Day in the Life Prep Amplifier™ for each one you contact.

DAY IN THE LIFE PREP AMPLIFIER

Name of the contact:
What are their social media handles?
LinkedIn: Twitter: Instagram: Facebook:
List other online/print sources: ***(Website, Glassdoor, Indeed, Search…)***
What topics are they discussing?
What are others saying about them?

DAY IN THE LIFE PREP AMPLIFIER (continued)

Questions to ask:

What is a day in the life like for a __________________ in the __________________ industry?

What challenges are you facing?

I am interviewing with ______________________. Have you heard of that company? Can you share any insights?

DAY IN THE LIFE PREP AMPLIFIER (continued)

Questions to ask:

What other questions do you have for your contact?

What questions for your interview does this conversation bring to mind?

The Question

You know the one. The question that you fear the most in an interview. You have a gap in your skills you hope they don't ask about. Or, you've had a gap in your employment history. Or maybe you have moved from job to job a lot at points in your career. Maybe you were only with your previous employer for a few months. You *hate* to answer that question. You *hope* it does not come up. When it does, you fumble for an answer. Your uncomfortableness shows like the coffee stain on your shirt you tried to get out before the interview.

Preparation, preparation, preparation. Write down your answer. Memorize it. Rehearse it. Rehearse it until it rolls off your tongue as naturally as your own name.

What is *the* question?

What is your answer?

After the Interview

Did you make a faux pas? Describe it:

What did you do to overcome it?

Thank-You Notes

List the individuals you met during the interview and a detail from the conversation to mention in your thank-you note:

11

The End Game

Success! You've Gotten the Offer

First, let's revisit your Top Ten Lists on your SOM Amplifier and complete an Offer Evaluation Amplifier.™

Lucky You! You Have Multiple Offers

Congratulations! As I always say, "A choice of one isn't really a choice at all." But now you have choices. Multiple offers have come in. Congratulations on each one!

Complete an Offer Evaluation Amplifier on each one.

Which offer wins based on points? ______________________________

How many number ones did it check off? ______________________________

Is there a clear winner in your gut? ______________________________

Compare the other components of the offer (salary, bonus, etc.).

Does one stand out over the others? ________

Divide the offers into three categories:

- **Negotiate.** These are the offers you definitely want to take to the next step.
- **Reject.** These offers are so far off the mark there is no way, even through negotiation, to make them viable.
- **Hold.** These offers you will do your best to keep "warm" while you negotiate with those in the first category.

OFFER EVALUATION AMPLIFIER

How many boxes does the position check?			
How about the company?		**The hiring manager?**	

Next to each of your Top Ten List items, check each one met by this company. Note the weighted score.

What about the other Top Ten Lists? Continue checking the boxes for the Next Position Next Boss Top Ten Lists.

How did they fare there? **What was their score:**

Company:		**Hiring Manager:**		**Position:**	

Other areas to consider:

Salary: How does the salary compare in the market?
Is it what you expected?

Other compensation:

Is there a bonus?		**Is it acceptable?**	

How is it determined?
Is it based on your performance or the performance of the company or both?

Benefits: *Healthcare covers and costs can vary widely. Be sure you understand the options.*

401(k)?		**401(k) matching?**		**Other profit sharing?**	

Other benefits: Vacation, flexible work schedule, work from home policy, other benefits

What parts of the offer would you like to negotiate?

Negotiate:

____

____

____

____

____

Hold:

____

____

____

____

____

Reject:

____

____

____

____

____

You Got the Job! Your Dream Job!

After you are done celebrating, there are still some things for you to do.
Send a note to the hiring manager.

Date sent: ____________________

Contact the other companies you were in negotiation with to tell them you have accepted an offer. Thank them very much for the time they invested in you and the process.

Company: ____________________ Date Sent: ____________________

Company: ____________________ Date Sent: ____________________

Company: ____________________ Date Sent: ____________________

Next, contact all the companies where you are actively interviewing. Thank them for their time.

Company: ______________________ Date Sent: ______________________

Company: ______________________ Date Sent: ______________________

Company: ______________________ Date Sent: ______________________

Send an update to everyone you networked with during this time. Tell them about your new role. Thank them for their help and support. Ask if there is anything you can do for them. If you have been sending a newsletter update to your network, you can use that to let people know and to thank them.

Name: ______________________ Date Sent: ______________________

Name: ______________________ Date Sent: ______________________

Name: ______________________ Date Sent: ______________________

Name: ______________________ Date Sent: ______________________

Name: ______________________ Date Sent: ______________________

Name: ______________________ Date Sent: ______________________

Name: ______________________ Date Sent: ______________________

Name: ______________________ Date Sent: ______________________

Name: ______________________ Date Sent: ______________________

Two Pledges

I, ____, promise to never let my network go cold!

Signed: ____

Date: ____

I, ____, promise to pay it forward. Whenever someone who is in transition reaches out to me for advice, I will meet with them.

Signed: ____

Date: ____

Oh, and one other thing. I would love to hear about your new dream job. Send me a note to

Jeff.Ton@TonEnterprisesLLC.com

I want to hear your story!

Date sent: ______________________

Bibliography

Barnaby, Jason. *Igniting the Fire Starter Within.* CreateSpace, 2019.

Waninger, Amy C. *Network beyond Bias: Making Diversity a Competitive Advantage for Your Career.* Lead at Any Level LLC, 2018.

Wood, Orrin G. *The Executive Job Search: A Comprehensive Handbook for Seasoned Professionals.* McGraw-Hill, 2003.

Yate, Martin. "How To Supercharge Your Resume." CareerCast.com, March 9, 2017. www.careercast.com/career-news/how-supercharge-your-resume.

Extra Amplifiers and Worksheets

On the following pages are additional copies of the Amplifier worksheets used throughout this workbook. If you need additional copies, you can download the PDFs at www.JeffreySTon.com/AYJS/Resources.

YOUR PERSONAL BRAND AMPLIFIER

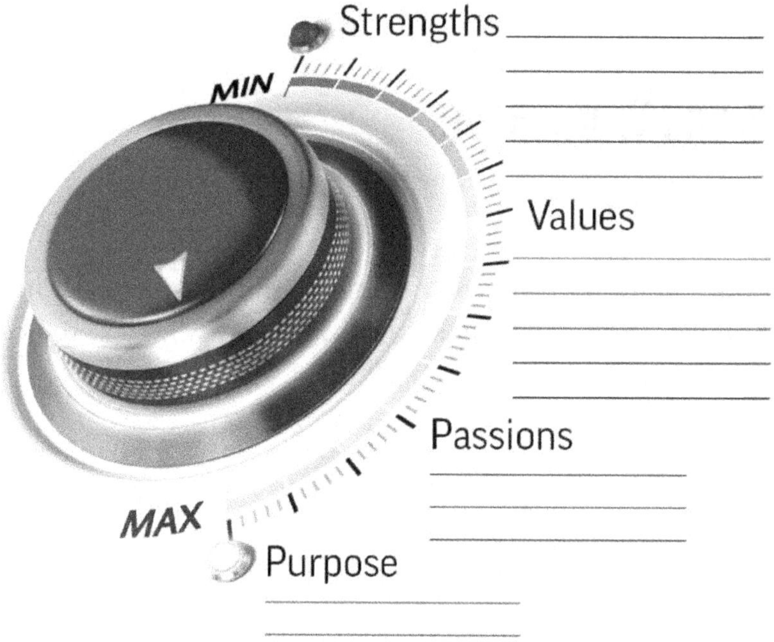

YOUR PERSONAL BRAND AMPLIFIER

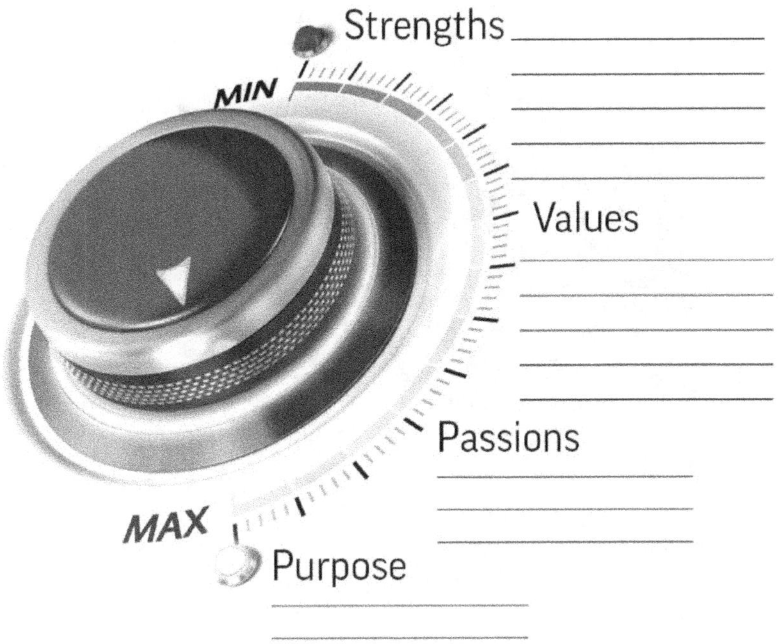

YOUR PERSONAL BRAND AMPLIFIER

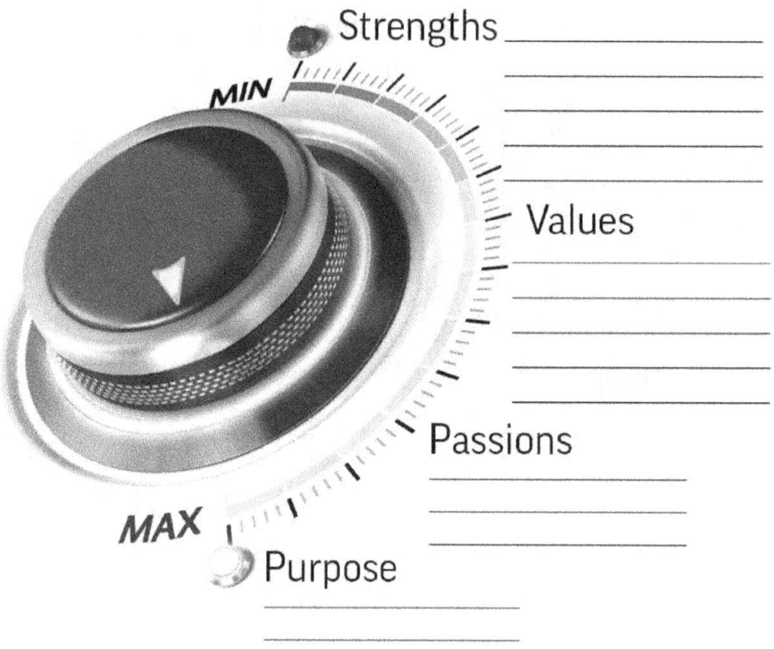

ACCOMPLISHMENT AMPLIFIER

START DATE	END DATE	COMPANY / ORGANIZATION	ROLE/TITLE	RESPONSIBILITIES	ACCOMPLISHMENTS	PROBLEM	ACTION	RESULTS

ACCOMPLISHMENT AMPLIFIER

START DATE	END DATE	COMPANY / ORGANIZATION	ROLE/TITLE	RESPONSIBILITIES	ACCOMPLISHMENTS	PROBLEM	ACTION	RESULTS

PAR ANALYSIS AMPLIFIER

PROBLEM:
ACTIONS:
RESULTS:
RESUME BULLET:
SKILLS USED:

PAR ANALYSIS AMPLIFIER

PROBLEM:
ACTIONS:
RESULTS:
RESUME BULLET:
SKILLS USED:

PAR ANALYSIS AMPLIFIER

PROBLEM:
ACTIONS:
RESULTS:
RESUME BULLET:
SKILLS USED:

PAR ANALYSIS AMPLIFIER

PROBLEM:
ACTIONS:
RESULTS:
RESUME BULLET:
SKILLS USED:

PAR ANALYSIS AMPLIFIER

PROBLEM:
ACTIONS:
RESULTS:
RESUME BULLET:
SKILLS USED:

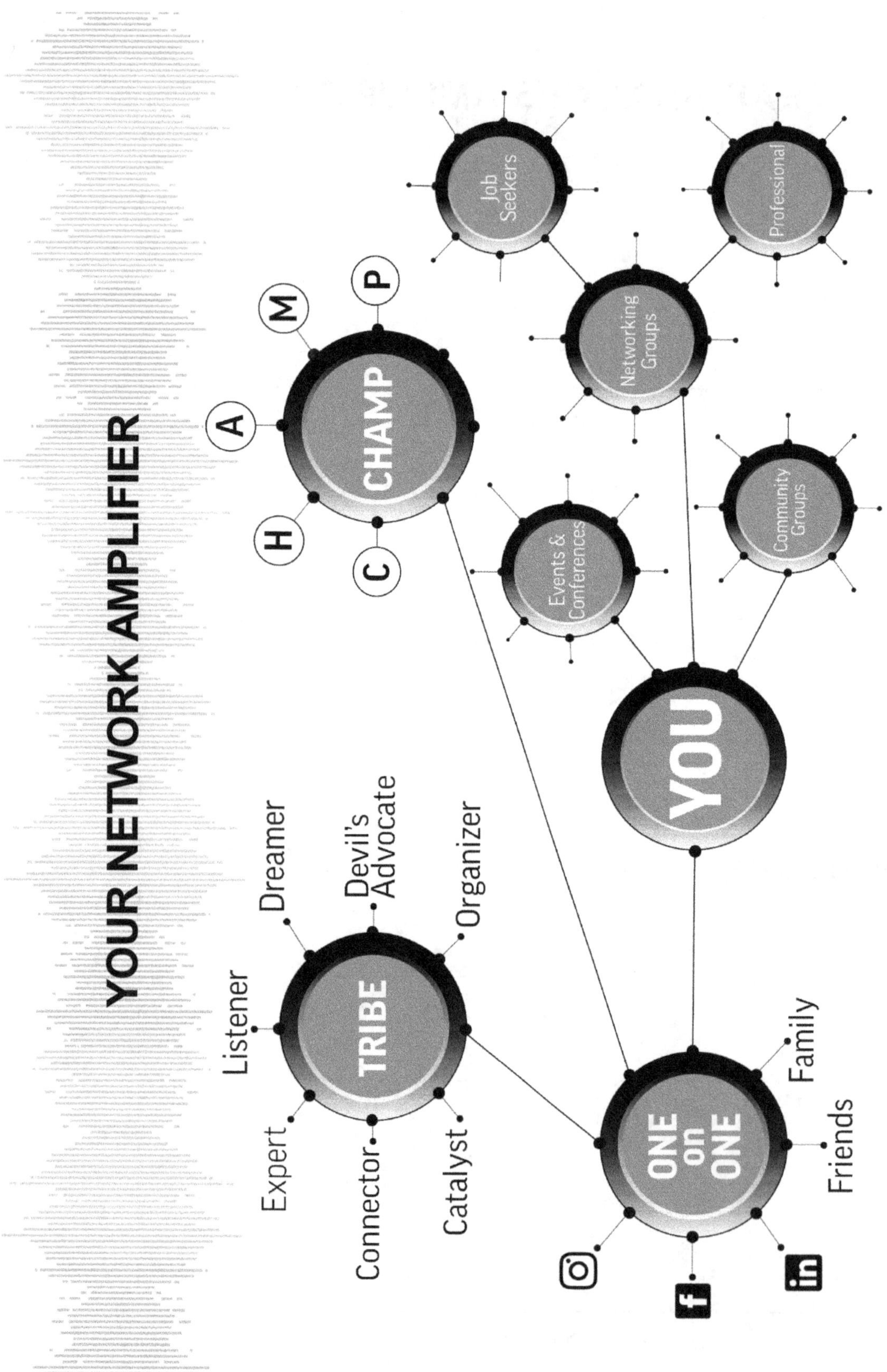
YOUR NETWORK AMPLIFIER
TRIBE
Listener
Dreamer
Devil's Advocate
Organizer
Catalyst
Connector
Expert
CHAMP
C
H
A
M
P
ONE on ONE
Family
Friends
YOU
Events & Conferences
Community Groups
Networking Groups
Job Seekers
Professional

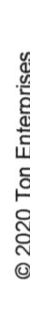

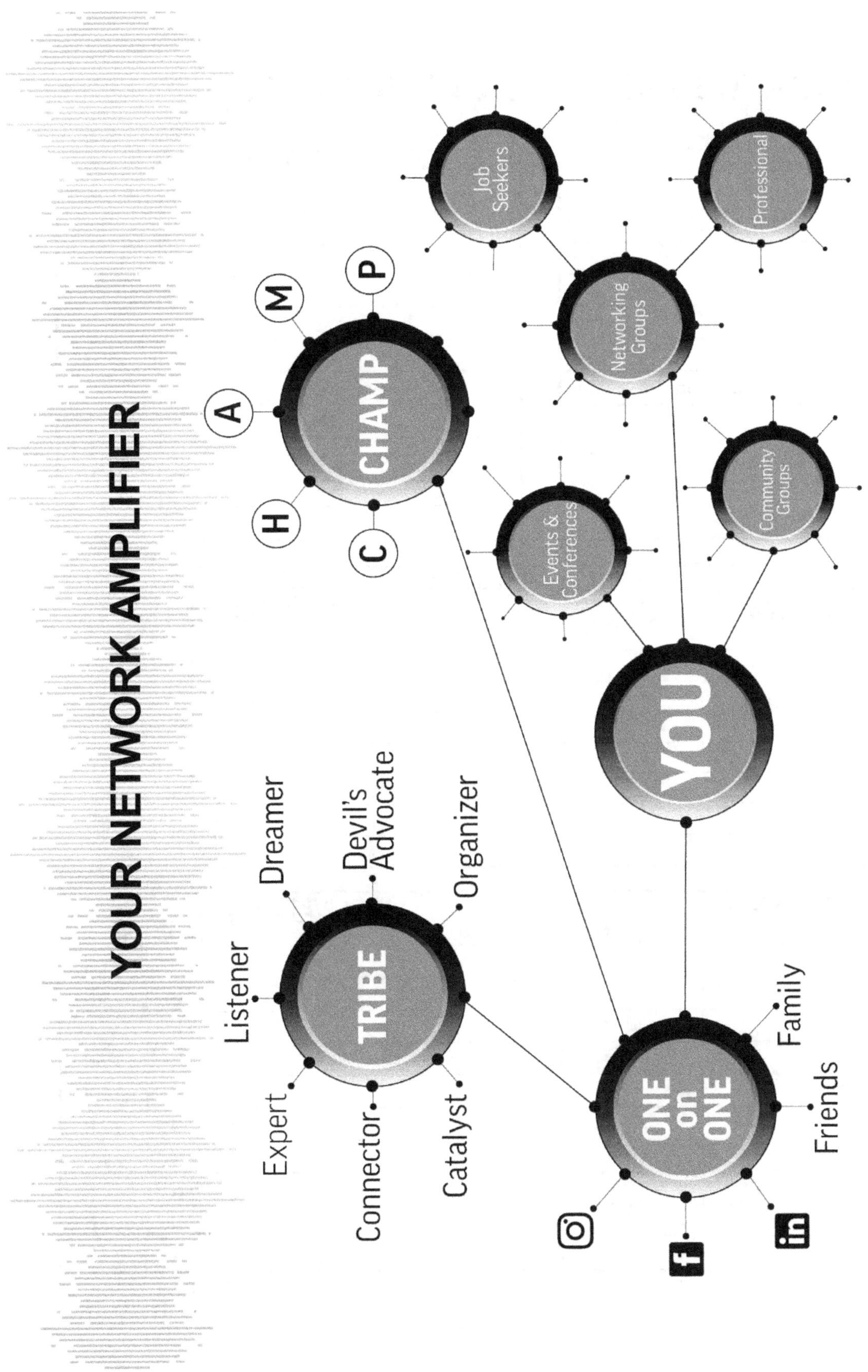

YOUR NETWORK AMPLIFIER
TRIBE
Listener
Dreamer
Devil's Advocate
Organizer
Catalyst
Connector
Expert
CHAMP
C
H
A
M
P
ONE on ONE
Family
Friends
YOU
Events & Conferences
Community Groups
Networking Groups
Job Seekers
Professional

RESUME AMPLIFIER WORKSHEET

TITLE
Target Job Description

SKILLS	
Skill	**Rank (0-5)**

Rank 0 = True Gap 5 = Rock Star

RESPONSIBILITIES		
Responsibility	**Yrs.**	**Desire (1-5)**

EXPERIENCES		
Experience	**Yrs.**	**# Acc.**

DELIVERABLES		
Deliverable	**Deliver**	**Sample**
	Y / N	Y / N
	Y / N	Y / N
	Y / N	Y / N
	Y / N	Y / N
	Y / N	Y / N
	Y / N	Y / N
	Y / N	Y / N
	Y / N	Y / N
	Y / N	Y / N
	Y / N	Y / N

RESUME AMPLIFIER WORKSHEET

TITLE

Target Job Description

SKILLS	
Skill	Rank (0-5)

Rank 0 = True Gap 5 = Rock Star

RESPONSIBILITIES		
Responsibility	Yrs.	Desire (1-5)

EXPERIENCES		
Experience	Yrs.	# Acc.

DELIVERABLES		
Deliverable	Deliver	Sample
	Y / N	Y / N
	Y / N	Y / N
	Y / N	Y / N
	Y / N	Y / N
	Y / N	Y / N
	Y / N	Y / N
	Y / N	Y / N
	Y / N	Y / N
	Y / N	Y / N
	Y / N	Y / N

SOM AMPLIFIER WORKSHEET

AMPLIFY YOUR JOB SEARCH • TOP TEN LISTS

NEXT POSITION	SCORE
☐	
☐	
☐	
☐	
☐	
☐	
☐	
☐	
☐	
☐	

NEXT BOSS	SCORE
☐	
☐	
☐	
☐	
☐	
☐	
☐	
☐	
☐	
☐	

NEXT COMPANY	SCORE
☐	
☐	
☐	
☐	
☐	
☐	
☐	
☐	
☐	
☐	

Each Top 10 List scores a max of 55 points.

SEARCH CRITERIA

FIELD	OPERATOR	VALUE

SOM AMPLIFIER WORKSHEET

AMPLIFY YOUR JOB SEARCH • TOP TEN LISTS

NEXT POSITION	SCORE
☐	
☐	
☐	
☐	
☐	
☐	
☐	
☐	
☐	
☐	

NEXT BOSS	SCORE
☐	
☐	
☐	
☐	
☐	
☐	
☐	
☐	
☐	
☐	

NEXT COMPANY	SCORE
☐	
☐	
☐	
☐	
☐	
☐	
☐	
☐	
☐	
☐	

Each Top 10 List scores a max of 55 points.

SEARCH CRITERIA

FIELD	OPERATOR	VALUE

INTERVIEW PREP AMPLIFIER

What is the name of the company asking for the interview?

What are their social media handles?

LinkedIn: Facebook:

Twitter: Other:

Instagram:

List other online/print sources: ***(Website, Glassdoor, Indeed, Search...)***

What topics are they discussing?

What are others saying about them?

What questions does that spark?

INTERVIEW PREP AMPLIFIER

What is the name of the company asking for the interview?	
What are their social media handles?	
LinkedIn:	Facebook:
Twitter:	Other:
Instagram:	
List other online/print sources: ***(Website, Glassdoor, Indeed, Search...)***	
What topics are they discussing?	
What are others saying about them?	
What questions does that spark?	

INTERVIEW PREP AMPLIFIER

What is the name of the company asking for the interview?

What are their social media handles?

LinkedIn: Facebook:

Twitter: Other:

Instagram:

List other online/print sources: ***(Website, Glassdoor, Indeed, Search...)***

What topics are they discussing?

What are others saying about them?

What questions does that spark?

INTERVIEW PREP AMPLIFIER

What is the name of the company asking for the interview?	
What are their social media handles?	
LinkedIn:	Facebook:
Twitter:	Other:
Instagram:	
List other online/print sources: ***(Website, Glassdoor, Indeed, Search...)***	
What topics are they discussing?	
What are others saying about them?	
What questions does that spark?	

INTERVIEW PREP AMPLIFIER

What is the name of the company asking for the interview?	
What are their social media handles?	
LinkedIn:	Facebook:
Twitter:	Other:
Instagram:	
List other online/print sources: ***(Website, Glassdoor, Indeed, Search...)***	
What topics are they discussing?	
What are others saying about them?	
What questions does that spark?	

INTERVIEWER PREP AMPLIFIER

Name of the Interviewer:
What are their social media handles?
LinkedIn: Twitter: Instagram: Facebook:
List other online/print sources: ***(Website, Glassdoor, Indeed, Search…)***
What topics are they discussing?
What are others saying about them?

INTERVIEWER PREP AMPLIFIER (continued)

How long have they been at the company?
How many people are they connected with at the company?
Where are they in the organization's hierarchy?
What does all of this say about their level of influence at the company?
What questions does your research spark?

INTERVIEWER PREP AMPLIFIER

Name of the Interviewer:

What are their social media handles?

LinkedIn:

Twitter:

Instagram:

Facebook:

List other online/print sources: ***(Website, Glassdoor, Indeed, Search...)***

What topics are they discussing?

What are others saying about them?

INTERVIEWER PREP AMPLIFIER (continued)

How long have they been at the company?
How many people are they connected with at the company?
Where are they in the organization's hierarchy?
What does all of this say about their level of influence at the company?
What questions does your research spark?

INTERVIEWER PREP AMPLIFIER

Name of the Interviewer:

What are their social media handles?

LinkedIn:

Twitter:

Instagram:

Facebook:

List other online/print sources: ***(Website, Glassdoor, Indeed, Search...)***

What topics are they discussing?

What are others saying about them?

INTERVIEWER PREP AMPLIFIER (continued)

How long have they been at the company?
How many people are they connected with at the company?
Where are they in the organization's hierarchy?
What does all of this say about their level of influence at the company?
What questions does your research spark?

INTERVIEWER PREP AMPLIFIER

Name of the Interviewer:
What are their social media handles?
LinkedIn: Twitter: Instagram: Facebook:
List other online/print sources: ***(Website, Glassdoor, Indeed, Search…)***
What topics are they discussing?
What are others saying about them?

INTERVIEWER PREP AMPLIFIER (continued)

How long have they been at the company?
How many people are they connected with at the company?
Where are they in the organization's hierarchy?
What does all of this say about their level of influence at the company?
What questions does your research spark?

INTERVIEWER PREP AMPLIFIER

Name of the Interviewer:
What are their social media handles?
LinkedIn: Twitter: Instagram: Facebook:
List other online/print sources: ***(Website, Glassdoor, Indeed, Search...)***
What topics are they discussing?
What are others saying about them?

INTERVIEWER PREP AMPLIFIER (continued)

How long have they been at the company?
How many people are they connected with at the company?
Where are they in the organization's hierarchy?
What does all of this say about their level of influence at the company?
What questions does your research spark?

COMPETITION PREP AMPLIFIER

(Complete a Competition Prep Amplifier for each Competitor)

What is the name of the company's competitor?	
What are their social media handles?	
LinkedIn:	Facebook:
Twitter:	Other:
Instagram:	
List other online/print sources: ***(Website, Glassdoor, Indeed, Search...)***	
What topics are they discussing?	
What are others saying about them?	
What questions does that spark?	

COMPETITION PREP AMPLIFIER

(Complete a Competition Prep Amplifier for each Competitor)

What is the name of the company's competitor?	
What are their social media handles?	
LinkedIn:	Facebook:
Twitter:	Other:
Instagram:	
List other online/print sources: ***(Website, Glassdoor, Indeed, Search…)***	
What topics are they discussing?	
What are others saying about them?	
What questions does that spark?	

COMPETITION PREP AMPLIFIER

(Complete a Competition Prep Amplifier for each Competitor)

What is the name of the company's competitor?	
What are their social media handles?	
LinkedIn:	Facebook:
Twitter:	Other:
Instagram:	
List other online/print sources: ***(Website, Glassdoor, Indeed, Search…)***	
What topics are they discussing?	
What are others saying about them?	
What questions does that spark?	

COMPETITION PREP AMPLIFIER

(Complete a Competition Prep Amplifier for each Competitor)

What is the name of the company's competitor?	
What are their social media handles?	
LinkedIn:	Facebook:
Twitter:	Other:
Instagram:	
List other online/print sources: ***(Website, Glassdoor, Indeed, Search…)***	
What topics are they discussing?	
What are others saying about them?	
What questions does that spark?	

COMPETITION PREP AMPLIFIER

(Complete a Competition Prep Amplifier for each Competitor)

What is the name of the company's competitor?	
What are their social media handles?	
LinkedIn:	Facebook:
Twitter:	Other:
Instagram:	
List other online/print sources: ***(Website, Glassdoor, Indeed, Search…)***	
What topics are they discussing?	
What are others saying about them?	
What questions does that spark?	

DAY IN THE LIFE PREP AMPLIFIER

Name of the contact:
What are their social media handles?
LinkedIn: Twitter: Instagram: Facebook:
List other online/print sources: ***(Website, Glassdoor, Indeed, Search…)***
What topics are they discussing?
What are others saying about them?

DAY IN THE LIFE PREP AMPLIFIER (continued)

Questions to ask:

What is a day in the life like for a __________________ in the __________________ industry?
What challenges are you facing?
I am interviewing with _____________________. Have you heard of that company? Can you share any insights?

DAY IN THE LIFE PREP AMPLIFIER (continued)

Questions to ask:

What other questions do you have for your contact?
What questions for your interview does this conversation bring to mind?

DAY IN THE LIFE PREP AMPLIFIER

Name of the contact:
What are their social media handles?
LinkedIn: Twitter: Instagram: Facebook:
List other online/print sources: ***(Website, Glassdoor, Indeed, Search…)***
What topics are they discussing?
What are others saying about them?

DAY IN THE LIFE PREP AMPLIFIER (continued)

Questions to ask:

What is a day in the life like for a ________________ in the ________________ industry?
What challenges are you facing?
I am interviewing with ___________________. Have you heard of that company? Can you share any insights?

DAY IN THE LIFE PREP AMPLIFIER (continued)

Questions to ask:

What other questions do you have for your contact?

What questions for your interview does this conversation bring to mind?

DAY IN THE LIFE PREP AMPLIFIER

Name of the contact:

What are their social media handles?

LinkedIn:

Twitter:

Instagram:

Facebook:

List other online/print sources: ***(Website, Glassdoor, Indeed, Search…)***

What topics are they discussing?

What are others saying about them?

DAY IN THE LIFE PREP AMPLIFIER (continued)

Questions to ask:

What is a day in the life like for a ____________________ in the ____________________ industry?
What challenges are you facing?
I am interviewing with ________________________. Have you heard of that company? Can you share any insights?

DAY IN THE LIFE PREP AMPLIFIER (continued)

Questions to ask:

What other questions do you have for your contact?

What questions for your interview does this conversation bring to mind?

DAY IN THE LIFE PREP AMPLIFIER

Name of the contact:

What are their social media handles?

LinkedIn:

Twitter:

Instagram:

Facebook:

List other online/print sources: ***(Website, Glassdoor, Indeed, Search…)***

What topics are they discussing?

What are others saying about them?

DAY IN THE LIFE PREP AMPLIFIER (continued)

Questions to ask:

What is a day in the life like for a ________________ in the ________________ industry?
What challenges are you facing?
I am interviewing with ____________________. Have you heard of that company? Can you share any insights?

DAY IN THE LIFE PREP AMPLIFIER (continued)

Questions to ask:

What other questions do you have for your contact?

What questions for your interview does this conversation bring to mind?

DAY IN THE LIFE PREP AMPLIFIER

Name of the contact:
What are their social media handles?
LinkedIn: Twitter: Instagram: Facebook:
List other online/print sources: ***(Website, Glassdoor, Indeed, Search…)***
What topics are they discussing?
What are others saying about them?

DAY IN THE LIFE PREP AMPLIFIER (continued)

Questions to ask:

What is a day in the life like for a ________________ in the ________________ industry?
What challenges are you facing?
I am interviewing with ____________________. Have you heard of that company? Can you share any insights?

DAY IN THE LIFE PREP AMPLIFIER (continued)

Questions to ask:

What other questions do you have for your contact?
What questions for your interview does this conversation bring to mind?

OFFER EVALUATION AMPLIFIER

How many boxes does the position check?			
How about the company?		**The hiring manager?**	

Next to each of your Top Ten List items, check each one met by this company. Note the weighted score.

What about the other Top Ten Lists? Continue checking the boxes for the Next Position Next Boss Top Ten Lists.

How did they fare there? **What was their score:**

Company:		**Hiring Manager:**		**Position:**	

Other areas to consider:

Salary: How does the salary compare in the market? Is it what you expected?					
Other compensation:					
Is there a bonus?		**Is it acceptable?**			
How is it determined? Is it based on your performance or the performance of the company or both?					
Benefits: *Healthcare covers and costs can vary widely. Be sure you understand the options.*					
401(k)?		**401(k) matching?**		**Other profit sharing?**	
Other benefits: Vacation, flexible work schedule, work from home policy, other benefits					
What parts of the offer would you like to negotiate?					

OFFER EVALUATION AMPLIFIER

How many boxes does the position check?			
How about the company?		**The hiring manager?**	

Next to each of your Top Ten List items, check each one met by this company. Note the weighted score.

What about the other Top Ten Lists? Continue checking the boxes for the Next Position Next Boss Top Ten Lists.

How did they fare there? **What was their score:**

Company:		**Hiring Manager:**		**Position:**	

Other areas to consider:

Salary: How does the salary compare in the market? **Is it what you expected?**

Other compensation:			
Is there a bonus?		**Is it acceptable?**	
How is it determined? **Is it based on your performance or the performance of the company or both?**			

Benefits: *Healthcare covers and costs can vary widely. Be sure you understand the options.*					
401(k)?		**401(k) matching?**		**Other profit sharing?**	
Other benefits: Vacation, flexible work schedule, work from home policy, other benefits					

What parts of the offer would you like to negotiate?

OFFER EVALUATION AMPLIFIER

How many boxes does the position check?			
How about the company?		**The hiring manager?**	

Next to each of your Top Ten List items, check each one met by this company. Note the weighted score.

What about the other Top Ten Lists? Continue checking the boxes for the Next Position Next Boss Top Ten Lists.

How did they fare there? **What was their score:**

Company:		**Hiring Manager:**		**Position:**	

Other areas to consider:

Salary: How does the salary compare in the market? Is it what you expected?					
Other compensation:					
Is there a bonus?		**Is it acceptable?**			
How is it determined? Is it based on your performance or the performance of the company or both?					
Benefits: *Healthcare covers and costs can vary widely. Be sure you understand the options.*					
401(k)?		**401(k) matching?**		**Other profit sharing?**	
Other benefits: Vacation, flexible work schedule, work from home policy, other benefits					
What parts of the offer would you like to negotiate?					

OFFER EVALUATION AMPLIFIER

How many boxes does the position check?					
How about the company?			**The hiring manager?**		
Next to each of your Top Ten List items, check each one met by this company. Note the weighted score. What about the other Top Ten Lists? Continue checking the boxes for the Next Position Next Boss Top Ten Lists. How did they fare there? **What was their score:**					
Company:		**Hiring Manager:**		**Position:**	

Other areas to consider:

Salary: How does the salary compare in the market? Is it what you expected?					
Other compensation:					
Is there a bonus?			**Is it acceptable?**		
How is it determined? Is it based on your performance or the performance of the company or both?					
Benefits: *Healthcare covers and costs can vary widely. Be sure you understand the options.*					
401(k)?		**401(k) matching?**		**Other profit sharing?**	
Other benefits: Vacation, flexible work schedule, work from home policy, other benefits					
What parts of the offer would you like to negotiate?					

OFFER EVALUATION AMPLIFIER

How many boxes does the position check?			
How about the company?		**The hiring manager?**	

Next to each of your Top Ten List items, check each one met by this company. Note the weighted score.

What about the other Top Ten Lists? Continue checking the boxes for the Next Position Next Boss Top Ten Lists.

How did they fare there? **What was their score:**

Company:		**Hiring Manager:**		**Position:**	

Other areas to consider:

Salary: How does the salary compare in the market?
Is it what you expected?

Other compensation:

Is there a bonus?		**Is it acceptable?**	

How is it determined?
Is it based on your performance or the performance of the company or both?

Benefits: *Healthcare covers and costs can vary widely. Be sure you understand the options.*

401(k)?		**401(k) matching?**		**Other profit sharing?**	

Other benefits: Vacation, flexible work schedule, work from home policy, other benefits

What parts of the offer would you like to negotiate?

OFFER EVALUATION AMPLIFIER

How many boxes does the position check?			
How about the company?		**The hiring manager?**	

Next to each of your Top Ten List items, check each one met by this company. Note the weighted score.

What about the other Top Ten Lists? Continue checking the boxes for the Next Position Next Boss Top Ten Lists.

How did they fare there? **What was their score:**

Company:		**Hiring Manager:**		**Position:**	

Other areas to consider:

Salary: How does the salary compare in the market?
Is it what you expected?

Other compensation:

Is there a bonus?		**Is it acceptable?**	

How is it determined?
Is it based on your performance or the performance of the company or both?

Benefits: *Healthcare covers and costs can vary widely. Be sure you understand the options.*

401(k)?		**401(k) matching?**		**Other profit sharing?**	

Other benefits: Vacation, flexible work schedule, work from home policy, other benefits

What parts of the offer would you like to negotiate?

About the Author

Jeff Ton is a sought-after leadership speaker, author, and explorer, having led powerful teams and built successful IT departments for over thirty years. He is the author of *Amplify Your Value* (2018) and hosts the podcast *Status Go*. As a frequent keynote speaker, he has explored topics related to the evolving IT landscape and the changing role of the CIO.

Jeff served in various roles with Thomson Multimedia (RCA) for over fourteen years. He then guided technology and business strategy as chief information officer for Lauth Property Group and later for Goodwill Industries of Central & Southern Indiana. Until early in 2020, Jeff was senior vice president of product and strategic alliances at InterVision. There he thrived on developing people while driving the company's product strategy, service vision, and strategic approach.

Throughout his career, Jeff has mentored, coached, and guided hundreds of professionals in their careers. His strategies of first looking to self, building a strong professional network, defining what makes a dream job, and then locating that dream job have enabled countless professionals to find their dream jobs.

Meet Jeff and learn more at www.JeffreySTon.com.

INSIGHTS

Jeffrey S Ton

SPEAKER - AUTHOR - EXPLORER

Join my weekly newsletter for thought-provoking insights delivered straight to your inbox every Tuesday! You'll receive:

- **Timely Musings:** Insights and lessons learned throughout the week
- **Readers' Q&A:** My response to someone's recent question
- **Success Spotlight:** Highlight of a person or company helping others grow
- **Rivers of Thought:** A more personal observation or musing on a topic

Subscribe Now

https://mailchi.mp/jeffreyston.com/leadershipinsights

Also by Jeffrey S. Ton

Amplify Your Value:
Leading IT with Strategic Vision

Are you an IT leader who struggles to make your voice heard? Does your company's executive team leave you out of important meetings? Are your business ideas and opinions never taken seriously? Keynote speaker and IT visionary Jeff Ton has thirty-five years of experience helping companies build strategic technology plans and innovative practices. His transformative methods will guide you and your department in transitioning from "the computer guys" to the heart of the business.

Amplify Your Value is a must-have reference for IT heads who are ready to take their leadership skills to the next level. If you like systematic action plans, innovative management, and real-world examples, then you'll love Jeff Ton's insightful guide.

Buy now at
https://jeffreyston.com/author-amplify-your-value

"Jeff tells a compelling story of being a CIO in the trenches—taking charge when opportunities present themselves, shoring up operations when required, and evolving strategies that drive business results. IT leaders will relate to his challenges and learn best practices from an experienced leader."

—Isaac Sacolick
President and CIO of StarCIO and
author of *Driving Digital*

www.ingramcontent.com/pod-product-compliance
Lightning Source LLC
Chambersburg PA
CBHW081111080526
44587CB00021B/3548
* 9 7 8 1 7 3 5 3 0 9 0 3 3 *